Flourishes *of* France

FROM AVIGNON TO STRASBOURG

A TRAVEL PHOTO ART BOOK

LAINE CUNNINGHAM

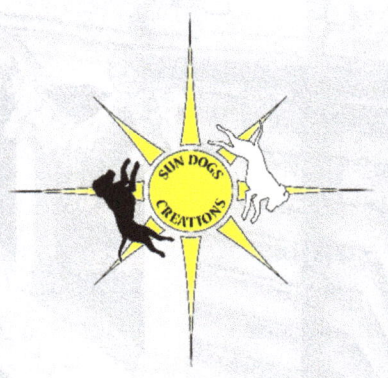

Flourishes of France

From Avignon to Strasbourg

A Travel Photo Art Book

Published by Sun Dogs Creations
Changing the World One Book at a Time
Print ISBN: 9781946732866

Cover Design by Angel Leya

Copyright © 2018 Laine Cunningham

All rights reserved. No part of this book may be reproduced in any form or by any means, electronic, mechanical, digital, photocopying or recording, except for the inclusion in a review, without permission in writing from the publisher.

THE TRAVEL PHOTO ART SERIES

Bikes of Berlin

Necropolises of New Orleans I & II

Ruins of Rome I & II

Ancients of Assisi I & II

Panoramas of Portugal

Nuances of New York

Glimpses of Germany

Impressions of Italy

Altitudes of the Alps

Coast of California

Utopia of the Unicorn

Knights Through the Ages

Portraits of Paris

COZY COTTAGE

LIMINAL

PANSIES

WEEP

BISHOP

ARTFUL

BEACON

FIELDSTONE

GATHERING

NO EXIT

OUTDOOR LIVING

BROODING

EASTER ISLAND

BENDING RAIN

FACES

BRIMFUL

BORDERS

TIDES

MATCHSTICKS

CHALK

MOOSE

LATE LIGHT

About the Author

Laine Cunningham's books take readers around the world. *The Family Made of Dust* is set in the Australian Outback, while *Reparation* is a novel of the American Great Plains. Her women's travel adventure memoir *Woman Alone: A Six-Month Journey Through the Australian Outback* appeals to fans of *Wild* and *Eat Pray Love*.

Fiction

The Family Made of Dust

Beloved

Reparation

Nonfiction

Woman Alone

On the Wallaby Track: Australian Words and Phrases

Seven Sisters: Messages from Aboriginal Australia

Writing While Female or Black or Gay

The Zen of Travel
The Zen of Gardening
Zen in the Stable
The Zen of Chocolate
The Zen of Dogs

The Wisdom of Puppies
The Wisdom of Babies
The Wisdom of Weddings

Bikes of Berlin
Ruins of Rome I & II
Necropolises of New Orleans I & II
Ancients of Assisi I & II
Panoramas of Portugal
Nuances of New York
Glimpses of Germany
Impressions of Italy
Coast of California
Altitudes of the Alps
Knights Through the Ages
Utopia of the Unicorn
Flourishes of France
Portraits of Paris

www.ingramcontent.com/pod-product-compliance
Lightning Source LLC
Chambersburg PA
CBHW041322110526
44591CB00021B/2876